# What Super Traders Don't Want You To Know

Azeez Mustapha

**ADVFN** BOOKS

# CONTENTS

# INTRODUCTION

This is a sequel to my recent book, *Learn from the Generals of the Markets.*

There are certain things that are known by super traders, but which aren't known by the general public. You will therefore benefit greatly from learning the principles that give super traders such a huge edge. It takes many years of dogged effort to reach consistent profitability in the markets, but if you don't want to reach profitability by trial and error (which takes many years and costs a lot of resources), you can reduce the learning curve significantly by learning the methods and principles some expert traders have used to become triumphant. This is the shortest way to break through.

In a recent interview in TRADERS' magazine (November 2014), Ian Cassel says: "Always surround yourself with people that are better than you. Your friends have far greater influence over your future than you think. If you want to be successful, start hanging out with successful people. If you want a better marriage, hang out with other couples that have a great marriage. Your life will change for the better."

How true is this statement! When you hang out with those who hate trading, those who have been floored by the markets and have sworn not to have anything to do with the markets again, those who are afraid of the challenges the markets offer, those whose job it is to discourage you from attaining your goals in life, then you can't become successful in the markets.

We need to surround ourselves with successful traders – or, at least, read about them and the principles that can be learned from them.

The super traders featured in this book will inspire you and reveal the principles behind their success.

# CHAPTER 1

# Steven Cohen:
## An Enigmatic Market Speculator

*"What you do not believe, you can never become." – Anonymous*

Born on 11 June 1956, Steven A Cohen is an American funds manager. He grew up in New York, where his parents worked. He began to play poker while still in high school – something that could have groomed him to develop a liking for the vagaries of the markets. When in school, he opened a brokerage account with some of his tuition fee. He got a degree in economics in 1978. After that, he was hired at Gruntal & Co in 1978 (a Wall Street firm). On his first day as a trader, he made a profit of eight thousand dollars. Later, he was making at least one hundred thousand dollars per day. In 1984, he was managing his own trading group at Gruntal. He founded his own firm, SAC Capital Advisors, in 1992 (with about twenty million dollars of his own money).

Steven has been very successful in his career. In 2005 he was paid one billion dollars as salary. In 2011, he was paid a salary of six hundred million dollars. As of March 2013, he was ranked as the one hundred and sixth richest individual on earth (number thirty-five in the States), being worth far above nine billion dollars. A Wall Street Journal article called him a hedge fund king. Time Magazine and Bloomberg Markets Magazine once ranked him among one of the most influential people. He has been married twice and has seven children. Unlike some billionaire funds managers who have donated huge amounts of money to charities, Steven is an avid lover of arts and has spent huge amounts of money on collecting artworks. Since 2000, he has spent hundreds of millions of dollars on his collection. He is constantly ranked among the top ten biggest-spending art collectors. That's how he prefers to spend his money.

**Lessons**

Here are some of the helpful things to learn from Steven:

1. There are some who can talk lots about trading and also trade successfully, while some can talk a lot about trading, but can't trade successfully. Steven rarely grants interviews. There are many people out there who don't talk, write or grant interview about trading, yet they constantly make killings in the markets.

2. It's been observed that at the beginning of one's trading career, one tends to favour short-term trades. However, as one gains more experience, one tends to hold one's trades longer than when one first started. This is exactly what happened to Steven, who at first didn't hold open trades for long periods of time. Later, he began to trade for the longer term.

3.  Teach your children the art of trading (as I explained my previous book, *Learn From the Generals of the Markets*). When they start having market-like experience while still a teenager, they usually grow up to become highly profitable traders. As far as the markets are concerned, there may be a seed of greatness in you and your children. Those who start trading when they are still young have the chance to become market wizards more easily than those who start when they are older. Steven began to experience the unpredictability of the markets while in high school. You can see what he later became.

4.  It's very important to stick to the industrial standards, rules and regulations in the course of one's career. No-one says you mustn't make money, as long as you're doing that legitimately. No doubt, Steven is a great trader, but sadly, he has been indicted in a large criminal insider trading scandal. It's believed that insider trading gives those who do it an unfair advantage over others. He was charged with failure to prevent insider trading in his company. Five of SAC Capital Advisors former employees were implicated and they admitted their guilt. More employees have also been charged. This is a serious allegation. Now US securities regulators are trying to bar Steven from managing other people's money. In fact, there have been many former funds managers who have been jailed, fined and disgraced because of insider trading. Steven's glorious and enviable career is mired in scandal. That should be a lesson to us.

**Conclusion**

Funds managers like Steven are worth our admiration because it's daunting to manage other peoples' money. It's far easier to manage one's own money. So it pays to get a trading methodology that fits your mindset and beliefs, for what fits you may not fit another person. When you use a methodology that agrees with your mindset, trading becomes much easier and enjoyable. Just make sure you have tested the methodology to make sure you like it. Tweak it and apply the rules as they fit you. Then make sure that the rules give you an edge. There's no end to acquisition of knowledge and maturity in the trading world.

This chapter concludes with a quote from Jesse Felder, who's also a money manager. He mentions the challenge of managing other people's money:

*"When trading your own account you can only harm yourself. When trading other people's money you have their financial future in your hands. My clients typically have most of their net worth invested with me and that's a major responsibility. I take it very seriously."* (Source: www.tradersonline-mag.com)

# CHAPTER 2

# Kenneth Fisher:
## Born to Be an Exceptional Expert Trader

*"Learn from failures, try again differently, fail, and try again. Your odds keep improving the more you try." – Kenneth L Fisher*

Kenneth L Fisher was born on 29 November 1950, in San Francisco, California, USA. He is the third and youngest son of Philip A Fisher, an astute investor who's also featured as a general of the markets in my last book, *Learn From the Generals of the Markets*.

Kenneth grew up in California and attended Humboldt State University where he got an economics degree. He then worked with his father before he started his own investment company (Fisher Investments) in 1979. In 2007, he went into partnership with Thomas

Grüner. He has been rewarded for maintaining independent thoughts in a world where people tend to harbour herd mentality. He has also won other notable awards.

Being an astute markets predictor, Kenneth has beaten the popular US markets for many years. He has authored several books. They are: *Super Stocks, The Wall Street Waltz, Minds that Made the Market, The Only Three Questions That Count, The Ten Roads to Riches, How to Smell a Rat, Debunkery* and *The Markets Never Forget.* Some of the books are bestsellers.

For many years, he has written numerous articles for top local and international financial magazines. With other concerned individuals, he has conducted extensive research in several areas of the financial industry. In 2011, he was among the 400 richest Americans (he was worth 1.7 billion dollars then). He is currently worth 1.9 billion dollars. His company manages more than 41 billion dollars for tens of thousands of customers (being the largest wealth manager in the States). He has been noted as one of the most influential people in the world of trading.

Kenneth's story can't be complete without mentioning his love and sacrifice for ecology and forestry. He has spent a great deal of time, energy and resources towards the cause which is his passion). He is married with three children. His official website is: Ken-fisher-investments.com.

**Lessons**

There are good lessons that can be learned from Kenneth. The best thing is to read his books and some of his innumerable articles. Some lessons are below:

1.  Like father, like son. Philip Fisher was a successful trader, and so is Kenneth Fisher, his son. The son is far richer than his dad,

who taught him the art of trading initially. Will you now teach your teens the art of trading? Certain successful traders today were taught the art of trading by their dads or uncles. Are you a successful trader? Then why can't you show your children the way? Or do you want them to start begging for jobs when they finish their university studies?

2. Trading will forever remain probabilistic in nature. It's never a game of certainties. Those who look for certainties are searching for what doesn't exist. Stop looking for certainties and start looking for how to control your risk.

3. Kenneth said speculation is two-thirds avoiding mistakes, one-third doing something right. Apply your trades flawlessly and stick to your rules. You're right only by trading according to your plans, not by being accurate in your forecasts.

4. According to Kenneth, professionals are terrible at forecasting bear markets. The media is worse. So why do you still think there are some who often predict the markets accurately?

5. Some people have to learn their lessons the hard way, not wanting to learn from others' mistakes, only from their own. Those who find it difficult to accept simple truths about trading will learn their lessons the hard way.

6. When the masses think a market is a great 'buy,' then it's time to sell it. When the public has too much confidence in a particular trading instrument, it's time to quit.

7. The best market to trade is the one the public has lost confidence in. When most people think a trading instrument is hopeless, then it's high time you were invested in it.

8. Kenneth once said that the developments in the markets tend to go contrary to the masses' expectation. Even if they are correct, it may be owing to a different cause than they think. It might even be accidental.

9. No matter how smart you are, no matter how intelligent or experienced you are, no matter what kind of strategy or combination of strategies you use, you can't be right every time. However, you can enjoy overall success in the markets, just as Kenneth has done.

10. The market is a good indicator of what's happening in an economy – whether the economy is good or bad.

**Conclusion**

Winston Churchill has been quoted as saying that it's easier to forecast what happened yesterday. Whatever happened in the past is historical in nature, and not an indicator of tomorrow's results. Prices aren't invariably error free and are discounted, and so far they are being determined by people. It doesn't matter the type of program and/or software used by them; the reality remains the same. Bear this in mind.

This chapter concludes with a quote by Kenneth:

*"Investors get overwhelmed by greed or fear but also forget that being greedy or fearful didn't work out for them in the past. But they also forget they were wrongly greedy or fearful because feelings now seem so much stronger (even though they're probably not)."*

# CHAPTER 3

# Jeff Cooper:
## A Trading Sharpshooter

*"Day trading strategies offer a shortcut in order to become profitable much quicker with a proven system." – Marcello Arrambide*

Jeff Cooper (not to be confused with another popular Jeff Cooper who was an American Marine and an expert on the use of small weapons) started trading in 1981 when he worked for his father who was managing funds at Drexel Burnham. Later, he left his dad to trade independently. Since then, he has become highly successful in making gains from the unpredictability of the markets. He has written great books titled *Hit and Run Trading I, Hit and Run Trading II* and *Hit and Run Lessons*. He has also released numerous educative materials for the benefits of beginners and advanced traders.

**Lessons**

Here are some lessons that can be learned from Jeff Cooper:

1.  Jeff fell in love with the art of trading and with the markets. Do you love/hate trading? Do you love/hate the markets? What makes you love/hate trading/markets? You can't make money from what you hate. For you to make it as a trader, you have to develop unending love for the markets.

2.  There was a battle sharpshooter named Jeff Cooper, and there's a trading sharpshooter named Jeff Cooper. The former was a US Marine and successful author on the use of small arms. The latter is a successful trader, market analyst, and an author of trading books.

3.  Jeff's dad trained him, although he also garnered trading principles that work from other great names in the trading world – you can see the quote below. You have to get imparted knowledge from great traders. This is one of the things that has helped me a lot.

4.  You don't need to be working in an office before you reach your financial freedom. Jeff trades in the comfort of his home in Malibu, California (overlooking the Pacific Ocean), where he also offers help to many traders the world over via the internet. Financial freedom is possible through trading.

5.  Day trading, swing trading, position trading and investing can be mastered according to the one that fits your personality. Jeff has mastered day trading and swing trading. In fact, he has one strategy called 'Opening Range Breakouts', which is a sort of Holy Grail to him. Whatever works for you – coupled with safe risk management – is your Holy Grail. This simply means losses

won't hurt your portfolio and gains will be moderately substantial.

6.  Trading since 1981 is no picnic. Serious traders take their career as a journey of a lifetime, not as a short-term stint. There are many types of financial markets that you can choose from.

**Conclusion**

The way to permanent victory in the markets is totally different than what most people would prefer. It's not an easy way. However, one can realise one's aims with the right mindset and simple but powerful trading principles. Beginner traders may flinch when told of what it takes to be a successful trader. One thing to note is that the ultimate goals in trading are far more worthwhile than the transitory effort that needs to be made to realize those goals.

This chapter concludes with a quote from Jeff:

*"…The works of WD Gann and Robert Prechter have inspired me more than anyone else. It was from their writings that I discovered cycles, patterns, and psychology dominate the market, and that the news breaks with the cycles, not the other way around."*

# CHAPTER 4

# Vladimir Ribakov:
## A Winning Signals Strategist

*"Most people don't understand that they need a trading system if they are to make money in the markets. Most importantly, that system must fit you, your objectives, your psychology, and your beliefs, for you to be able to trade it effectively." – Dr Van K Tharp*

Vladimir Ribakov is a renowned expert trader, mentor, signals provider, blogger, author, trading software developer and funds manager. He has his roots in the part of the world that used to be called the USSR. For many years, he has been handling the uncertainty in the currencies exchange markets and commodities markets victoriously.

Having achieved success in trading, he decided to reach out to those who need help – those livid and exasperated souls who long to make gains from the markets. Most of these people were misled into adopting various suicide trading principles in the past, and they suffered as a result of this. Vlad has endeavoured to assist some of those people in learning and applying winning trading principles and the results have been wonderful. Vlad's websites are Vladimirforexsignals.com, and Vladimirribakov.com. On those websites, you may want to tap into his peerless knowledge and experience. You can also access his trading signals, strategies, blog posts, ebooks, etc. All these are constantly updated. He has released some free helpful trading software like Spread Detector and so on. Spread Detector helps you determine when your broker widens the spread unfairly or according to their terms and conditions. It also helps you see whether a broker really has fixed spreads if they promise that.

One good way to learn from Vlad is to download his free ebooks that reveal important trading secrets. Those ebooks ought to come at a price, but the author really wants to help as many people as possible. His free ebooks are *The Secret Meaning of Japanese Candlesticks Part 1, The Secret Meaning of Japanese Candlesticks Part 2, What Type of Traders Do You Want to Be?, Psychological Trading and Money Management System* and *Converting Knowledge Into Practice.* His premium ebooks are titled *Sell the Rally, Buy the Valley* and *Profitable Trading Mind.*

## Lessons

The best way to learn from Vlad is to download his free ebooks and subscribe to his free trading signals. In addition, these are some of the lessons you can learn from him:

1.  The easiest and the quickest way to become a successful trader is to follow a winning trader's buy and sell recommendations –

with physical stops, targets, trade management and risk control. One pitfall is that most people aren't disciplined enough to follow the signal provider's recommendations as originally intended. Yet, they blame the signals provider. This also explains why many people purchase profitable trading strategies and still receive margin calls with them: the systems either don't fit them or they don't stick to the rules of the strategies.

2. Vlad himself declares: "I constantly scan the web for new systems, strategies and Forex services. I have to admit, there is a lot of crap out there but still, I have managed to find here and there interesting systems that actually work nicely. Sometimes I even test how to integrate them with my strategies and tools, to dramatically improve system performance." There are great trading strategies out there. Do you have a winning trading strategy? Vlad's winning strategies are Divergence Trading Method, Forex LST System (LST stands for: Learn, Simulate, Trade), etc. You can learn how to use those strategies from him.

3. Real winning traders should publish their genuine trading results. In the past, I mentioned some expert speculators who publish their track records for people to see. There are many people who claim to know much about online trading, but when you ask them for their track records, they can't show it. This is because they don't have track records. They know much about trading, but they can't make consistent gains. Vladimir is one of those rare breeds who make their track records public. This means that if you have followed his trading signals to the letter, you would have achieved the same results as he did.

4. However, you should know that good trading methods have winning and losing phases. The real thing is to have average winners that are much bigger than average losers over a long period of time. Personally, I've seen that a losing phase may hold

out longer than an average trader expects. I can experience this phase for up to four months in a year, but I manage my risk effectively, avoiding large drawdowns, and still coming out ahead at the end of the year (no matter how small the positivity may be). There's no way around this truth; you got to accept this or go do something else.

5.  Make your chart as simple as possible. It's awful to see how many traders use complicated trading techniques (and in reality, complicated trading techniques don't make more money than simple ones). The real secret to the Holy Grail is in using a positive expectancy strategy and controlling yourself and your risk. Please clean up your chart, and make your life easy. Why should you put too many indicators, custom indicators, bots and semi-automated systems, all on one chart? Your chart doesn't need to look like Michelangelo's paintings before you can become triumphant. Clean up your chart and keep things simple. KISS.

6.  Some year ago, Vlad published an article called *Brokers Horror Stories*. There are good brokers out there, and there are bad brokers. The kind of broker you choose will also play a big factor in your success or failure as a trader. Good brokers make sure that their clients experience excellent services and customer support; and merely one or two disgruntled clients don't really make them skunks (for no company is perfect). According to Vlad, some of the factors you need to consider before choosing a broker are: 1) Being authorized and regulated in the country where they have office, 2) Excellent customer support, 3) Competitive spreads, 4) Having been used and trusted by someone you know personally, 5) Meritorious awards, 6) Many accounts, funding and withdrawal options, 7) Being around for years, 8) Generous promos and so on.

## Conclusion

Unsuccessful traders seek help because they lose consistently after approaching those who call themselves markets gurus. You can't be a winning trader without learning what it takes to be a winning trader. Imagine starting your boxing career by challenging a world heavyweight champion. You know what the outcome will be, don't you? Really, current heavyweight champions started somewhere; as they envied the heavyweight champions of those days. The trick in trading success is to practice winning trading methods over and over again, until it becomes your second nature, although no methods works 100% of the time. Effective trading principles always work.

This chapter concludes with a quote from Vlad:

*"Like love, trading is an international language."*

# CHAPTER 5

# Toni Turner:
## A Happy Market Player

*"Always remember this: There are traders that have ruined entire accounts but still did not give up and were ultimately successful." – Marko Graenitz*

Toni Turner, a happy American trader, is a trading educator and a successful author of many trading and investment books. Some of the books are *A Beginner's Guide to Day Trading Online, A Beginner's Guide to Short Term Trading* and *Short-Term Trading in the New Stock Market.* These books are best-sellers and they've been translated into some Asian languages. She is in high demand as a financial expert at trading forums, expos, money shows and conferences throughout the US. She regularly appears on investment programs on TV channels and other media. Her main goal has been to show traders and investors how to become victorious market players.

Toni is very good at presenting difficult subjects in easy-to-understand formats for her students and clients. Being a great chart analyst, countless numbers of people have really benefitted from her opinions on the markets. One extremely grateful student admitted that one of Toni's workshops has really helped them to become a better trader and make more profits. She really cares for her students and clients. Toni is the President of TrendStar Group, Inc. Her official website is: http://www.toniturner.com.

## Lessons

To learn from Toni, you will need to join her online webinars, attend her seminars/workshops, attend conferences or money shows where she is also a featured guest, or buy some of her books. Here are a few of the lessons one can learn from Toni:

1.  What do you do in an overbought or oversold market when you're in a right direction? When you think the market is overbought or oversold, you can take your profits, or take a partial profit, or set your breakeven stop and then trailing stop (if you're a trend follower).

2.  There are trading instruments that speculators can watch as leading indicators of the broader markets. One of them is iShares Russell 2000 ETF ($IWM). When these leading indicators go south, it may mean that bears reign. When they go up, it may mean that bulls reign. According to Toni, when we see higher volume on a pullback in the context of an uptrend – higher volume than there was on the prior move up – it indicates that there are more sellers out there on the move down than there were buyers during the move up. When we see higher volume on a rally in the context of a downtrend – higher volume than there

was on the prior move up – it indicates that there are more buyers out there on the move up than there were sellers during the move down.

3.  It is agreed that most lose money because they think they must always be right. This either makes them risk too much or run their losses for as long as possible. Whenever you open new positions, you should know where you want to exit, either for profit or for loss. Losses ought not to be run.

4.  Toni Turner is a happy trader. If you Google her images or see her pictures in most cases, you'll see a happy trader, full of smiles. By doing the right things in the market, learning what it takes to be victorious in the markets, finding your purpose as a trader, and realizing your goal, you too can be happy. One doesn't need to always frown or be sad or full of worry as a result of the vagaries of the markets. You can always be a happy trader.

## Conclusion

Many wizards who began trading many decades ago know that rock-solid discipline and self-restraint were the most difficult things for traders to achieve. This is not something that can be achieved with ease, since it takes some serious determination. You trade to make money. Your gains are your reward for staking your money in the markets. Your gains are your reward for doing the right thing on the markets, for knowing what it takes to be successful, and for your rock-solid discipline.

This chapter is concluded by a quote from Toni Turner:

*"…For day traders, I think the recent volatility is a great opportunity to earn short-term gains."*

# CHAPTER 6

# Jaffray Woodriff:
## A Money Doubler?

*"I have found that when my primary goal is to trade well, I regularly experience moments of flow. I have also found that when my primary goal is to simply trade well, my results are better as a consequence." – Dr. Ken Long*

Born in 1969, Jaffray Woodriff is an American trader. He is CEO of Quantitative Investment Management (QIM), which he co-founded with Michael Geismar in 2003. He spent his childhood in Charlottesville, Virginia, and went to the University of Virginia. He largely taught himself the art of trading, having formed a desire to be a trader in a unique way with computer programs; he achieved unique results.

He has been referred to as one of the biggest hedge fund managers. His firm manages more than $4 billion but has only 32 employees. With an income of $90 million, he has been listed by Forbes as one of the highest paid funds managers. He is featured in Jack Schwager's 'Hedge Fund Market Wizards.'

Jaffray is married with two children, and he likes to play squash. He writes articles about various interesting trading topics.

## Lessons

These are some of the lessons that can be learned from Jaffray:

1. While some successful traders have been trained and groomed by other professionals, there are other self-taught traders like Jaffray Woodriff. Discovering what it takes to be a successful trader by trial and error isn't an easy thing.

2. Jaffray has had rough/tough times in the past. Since he didn't give up, he is now enjoying success in the markets. Are you experiencing any rough/tough times in the markets? Please don't give up; day by day, your breakthrough comes nearer.

3. He is proof that computer programs can make money for people in the markets. Yes, reliable auto trading programs can help one reach one's financial freedom providing that one programs sensible risk controls and positive expectancy rules into them.

4. Is Jaffray a money doubler? Far from it. He simple makes decent but consistent annual returns in the markets. Sometimes he may make 30% or 20% or even 18% (or more or less) per annum. The most important thing is that he makes money each year. His firm doesn't double accounts in weeks or months as many people would prefer. The thoughts that most people have about trading are wrong indeed. For you to double your account, you

need to bet too big. However, those who risk less tend to make more money than those who risk more. Those who risk less tend to survive bad markets more than those who risk more. The fastest way up may also be the fastest way down.

5.  Sometimes, a combination of good trading methodologies can generate better results that just using one good trading methodology.

6.  It is better or safer to test a trading idea in simulation mode before one applies it on real account.

7.  Tradable setups often appear in the markets over and over again. Historical data contains this as well. This means that trading methodologies that work don't change with the time and changing market conditions.

## Conclusion

When using a trading approach, more is made if one rides one's gains when one happens to be right. When the price seems overbought, some would expect it to reverse sharply. In most cases, the reversals that occur are temporary. What you think is overbought can still go far further upwards. This fact may seem impossible, but it often happens that the price that has gone in one's favour by 1,000 points can still go further upwards by another 1,000 points (it may even go further than that). This isn't a new thing.

This chapter is concluded with a quote from Jaffray:

*"...If you are trading the system, and it is not performing in line with expectations over some reasonable time frame, look for overfit and hindsight errors. If you are expecting a Sharpe ratio above 1, and you are getting a Sharpe ratio under 0.3, it means that you have made one or more important hindsight errors, or badly misjudged trading costs..."*

# CHAPTER 7

# Ray Dalio:
## The Steve Jobs of Investing

*"We are easily deceived when we are told exactly what we want to hear."* –
*Malcolm Robinson*

Ray Dalio was born on 1 August 1949, in Jackson Heights, Queens, New York, United States. He is an American hedge fund guru. Being a son of an artiste (the only child of his parents), he began to deal with the markets at the age of 12. He has both a BA and an MBA from reputable universities.

After his university experience, he worked at NYSE. Then he worked as director of commodities at Dominick & Dominick LLC; after which he was both a broker and trader at Shearson Hayden Stone. In 1974, he founded an investment firm named Bridgewater Associates. This firm has been playing the markets triumphantly since then. In 2012, it became the largest investment firm in the world, with assets that were worth $120 billion. His firm's website is Bwater.com.

In 2007, Ray accurately forecasted the credit crunch – which his firm survived with profits. Since he was worth $10 billion, he was named the 31st richest person in the USA (88th in the world), in March 2012. In the recent years, top magazines have included him in the list of the world's most influential people.

He lives in Greenwich, Connecticut. He is married and has four children.

**Lessons**

Here are some of the great trading lessons that can be learned from Ray:

1.  Ray Dalio is one of the richest hedge funds managers on this planet, yet his firm's performances are not always great. There were years he made good profits, and there were a few years in which the results were either small negativity (which was easily recovered), flat or breakeven. Despite this, he stands firm as an investor. Do you quit trading when your performances don't go according to your expectation? Do you abandon your good strategy during periods of flat performances, fleeting negativity or results that are below expectations? This isn't the right action to take; for all strategies, whether manual, semi-automated or automated, will eventually experience the aforementioned phases, but good ones will soon resume bringing profits. Bad market conditions may try hard to discourage you and wreck your determination. Sadly, the trading course is littered with those who had a determined start but did not keep going. Negative

thoughts may haunt you, but you'll stand firm and stick to your goals.

2.   It's best to accept that your trading methods don't know what will happen in the future. This will enable you to take measures that can safeguard your portfolios in worst-case scenarios. Traders that do well are those who accept that the future can't be predicted.

3.   It's better to be active in the markets than to be reactive. It's great for traders to trade in the moment. The markets – just like an economy – aren't that complicated unless we make them so for ourselves.

4.   According to Ray, one of the biggest problems facing traders is ego sensitivity which prevents us from working on our weaknesses and encouraging our strengths. Traders who want success should do the opposite.

5.   One journalist wrote that in spite of the fact that the euro was once dropping like a stone and the markets went maniacal, Ray was able to discuss mosquitoes at that moment. There are many things Ray is interested in (like meditation) apart from markets. Don't be occupied only by the markets, there's life outside trading. Trade and prosper, but don't forget to enjoy other aspect of life.

6.   Bridgewater once made around 13% per annum for about 19 years: sometimes 9.4%, sometimes 11%, or sometimes 2%. Hear me, greedy traders, gamblers and money-doublers, do you need to make hundreds of percentage per annum to be called successful? If you think so, well, it's possible, but I doubt if you can enjoy lasting success in the markets with that approach.

7.  Like Malcolm who's quoted above, people are really harmed when they are told what they want to hear. What can help people are the truths they may not want to hear. Ray believes that a notion that's a brutal honesty, no matter how uncomfortable, yields the best results. He once commented that telling him what he wanted to hear created sugar addition. There's no need to shy away from the truth because truthfulness is mandatory when it comes to independent thoughts and useful knowledge. In my books about traders, I've been making attempts to reveal the truths about trading; albeit with blatant honesty. Illusions and fantasies that others peddle can't help you.

8.  Even if your grades were poor while at school, you can still become great in life. You can still become a successful trader. Ray said he was a very ordinary kid who was a substandard high school student.

9.  As I have said before, it pays to be exposed to the markets when one is very young. When you become older, you'll find the art of speculation easier. Ray started speculating when he was 12. Then he purchased some Northeast Airlines shares for $300 and he later made over 200%.

10. If you are successful in the markets, please share your lessons with other traders so that they can benefit too. After past hesitation, Ray Dalio has started sharing his trading secrets. There are many frustrated traders out there who need our help. Please let's try to help them. If you have killer trading secrets which have made you very rich, they won't be useful for you in your grave. Please let the world benefit from the secrets.

11. Ray says: "In return, society rewards those who give it what it wants. That is why how much money people have earned is a rough measure of how much they gave society what it wanted."

Ray's foundation is helping many organizations. If you are rich, you can learn from that.

## Conclusion

We appreciate experts who started the trading race before us and just continually, consistently, steadily kept running until they passed on. Others started trading before us and they are still trading now. We must determine to keep going until we reach permanent financial freedom. There will be distractions and challenges from time to time. There will be instances along the way when the markets seem to 'disappoint' us, but we will be rewarded if we remain steadfast.

This chapter is concluded with a quote from Ray Dalio:

*"I worry about another leg down in the economies causing social disruption because deleveragings can be very painful – it depends on how they're managed."*

# CHAPTER 8

# Leda Braga:
## A High Earning Hedge Fund Manager

*"I'd never work for anyone else again. Plus, I love what I do."* – Dr Van K
*Tharp (Trading specialist)*

Leda Braga, a female trader, is one of the highest paid funds mangers
in the world. Holding a PhD in engineering, she is the president of
BlueCrest Capital Management (which was founded by Williams
Reeves and Michael Platt in 2000). The firm has offices in a number
of counties.

Leda manages the firm's biggest portfolio which is worth $16 billion,
using a proprietary trend-following approach. BlueCrest itself has a
total of $37 billion as a portfolio. She is an active researcher; always

looking for better investment opportunities and strategies. She has gained an estimated 16.67% per annum since 2005, and has personally earned about $5 million as a result of her trading activities.

Her firm's official website is: Bluecrestcapital.com.

**Lessons**

Here are some of the lessons that can be learned from Leda:

1.  Leda uses trend-following approaches to tackle the markets, which means that trend-following methods work.

2.  No trading method is perfect. The portfolio managed by Leda sometimes reaches break-even or flat performance. When your trading method performs below expectation, you'd need to take it as a normal thing. It happens to expert traders as well, so it doesn't mean you're not a good trader.

3.  Leda first worked as a lecturer and researcher before she inadvertently dived into the ocean of trading. She has never regretted her decision. Before she joined BlueCrest, she didn't place real trades (though she'd been exposed to the markets). No matter what you're currently doing for a living or as a hobby, you have the potential to become a great trader. The seed is in you. The fact that you've not placed real trades yet doesn't mean you can't be a great trader in future. Trading will become more and more interesting in future, and you merely need to adapt so that you can survive. Many talented students with mathematical and scientific backgrounds are showing interest in trading and hedge fund world. They can certainly make great contributions to trading. This profession is highly competitive and hard. Therefore you must find ways to become better than others and have an edge.

4.    According to one source, Leda's passion is the continual testing and refining of selected trading systems. Her firm emphasizes research and analysis. If you have great trading systems, you might want to find ways to improve them. No matter how good you are at trading, there's always room for improvement.

5.    Mighty oaks from little acorns grow. There was a time when BlueCrest's fund was only $300 million; now it's worth $37 billion. Try to be successful on smaller accounts first, then you may be worthy to handle much larger accounts. Your success with smaller portfolios will surely take you to greater heights.

6.    Technological advancement has made trading more enjoyable. There have been structural changes in the markets, including the way traders speculate. There is more transparency and better quotes. Electronic trading has been a boon to serious traders.

7.    Leda thinks that technology will keep on playing a vital role in the trading world. She forecasts that in future, science and technology will have a great influence on trading.

8.    Should funds managers try emerging markets? Yes, but they need to weigh their pros and cons. There are good market names in South America, Africa and Asia. These markets should be watched for excellent investing and trading opportunities, for they will become very attractive as they grow and stabilize. But there are some hitches to be wary of: tradable products, changing regulations, liquidity, opening/closing hours, sizes limitations and other restrictions. Truly, regulations on emerging markets keep changing; just like a highway code that keeps changing while one is driving, it makes safe driving difficult. You must make sure you know what you're doing – most traders don't.

## Conclusion

Author Dennis Fisher wrote that at the first battle of the Marne during the First World War, French lieutenant general Ferdinand Foch sent out a communiqué saying: "My centre is giving way, my right is retreating. Situation excellent. I am attacking." Dennis went on to say that the lieutenant general's willingness to see hope in a tough situation eventually led to victory for his troops. (Our Daily Bread, 4 January 2014). You may even experience negativity with your first trade ever, yet you can become a good trader in future. Many experienced pros can testify that they've been trading for 40 or 50 years and they still love the markets. There will be the trial of our commitment to trading success; it happens to the pros of the markets, and it will happen to us. The markets are full of rewarding experiences that can satisfy our hearts and make us happy, rich and good examples in the trading industry.

Leda Braga, who believes that the basis of successful trading is backed up by mathematical justification, says white box trading is better than black box trading. Her quote ends this chapter:

*"We're actually a white box, the white of the mind. We are fully auditable. If you are a pension fund with long-term liabilities, you want some reassurance that the business is sustainable. The hedge fund business is filled with very talented people, but talented people retire. What we do, this effort to articulate the investment process through algorithms, though equations, through code, means that the intellectual property exists in its own right. If I disappear tomorrow, it's fine."*

# CHAPTER 9

# Peter Lynch:
## What's So Special About
## This Market Maven?

*"Over the years I have benefitted from many traders (alive and dead), investors and professionals." – Alan Saunders*

Born on 19 January 1944, in Newton, Massachusetts, USA, Peter Lynch is considered to be one of the greatest investors around. He studied at Boston College (1965) and bagged his MBA from the Wharton School of the University of Pennsylvania (1968).

In 1966, he started working at Fidelity Investments. He began to keep tabs on key industries and eventually became the firm's director. He later became head of Magellan Fund which was worth $18 million

(1977). That portfolio had been increased to over $14 billion by the time he stopped managing the fund in 1990. From 1977 to 1990, he was making about 29.2% per annum. He beat the S&P 500 Index benchmark many times. In mutual funds, he emerged as the best earners of return in 2003. Indeed, his stakes on popular stocks have paid off and he is considered a legendary trader.

He has co-authored best sellers *One Up on Wall Street, Beating the Street* and *Learn to Earn*. The books are indeed a great help to anyone who wishes to attain success in the markets. He wrote many premium articles for Worth magazine.

Peter Lynch is a philanthropist who's donated huge amounts of money to causes he believes in.

## Lessons

These are the lessons that can be learned from Peter:

1. An individual trader is capable of making more money than professional traders, like Richard Dennis' Turtles and Lex van Dam's BBC Million Dollar traders were able to demonstrate. Your simple trading idea can make you rich in future.

2. Sometimes, it pays to employ a flexible investment style that adapts to changing market conditions. That's what Peter did.

3. Predicting future market conditions is like flogging a dead horse. It just won't work. Just try to capitalize on your gains and truncate your losses. If you wanted to predict the future, you might want to flip a coin to do that. In addition, if you can make extensive research, you're bound to sight great trading opportunities.

4.   Enter good trades and manage your positions well. It's sensible to have valid reasons for opening trades. Peter was a position trader who was not affected by transient market noises.

5.   Peter said there will always be something to worry about, and that's enough. Good traders have conquered their ego before they conquer the markets. We need to be humble enough to learn from our mistakes.

6.   Open only trades that you can handle. Too many trades with big position sizes can make you lose control.

7.   Looking for 90% accuracy in the market is far-fetched, but skilled traders can achieve about 60% accuracy. There's no perfect outcome in trading and if you don't want to see any minus in your trades, you're already a flop. Profitable trading is realized when losses are dealt with triumphantly.

8.   You don't need a PhD in math before you can be a great trader. An elementary school math is sufficient for you to deal with the markets.

9.   No-one is born with trading skills. The skills are only acquired through hard work and self-control. Yes, trading is a skill you can learn and master.

10.  The best trading approach is the simplest trading approach. Many market wizards use simple strategies and Peter is one of them. An easy trading approach would cause you to make the least amount of mistakes, whereas hard trading systems would cause you to fall into many errors. Simple trading systems are easier to understand and use in making good choices.

## Conclusion

Nowadays, speculation proffers chances of harnessing gains, but you need a working trading method to locate high-flying instruments. It may be difficult while trying to wait until you see your preferred setups, but as a speculator you need to accept that, for it's been proven that patience is rewarding.

This chapter is concluded with a quote from Peter:

*"Investing without research is like playing stud poker and never looking at the cards... If you stay half-alert, you can pick the spectacular performers right from your place of business or out of the neighbourhood shopping mall, and long before Wall Street discovers them."*

# CHAPTER 10

# Eddie Lampert:
## How He Made Billions of Dollars from the Markets

*"I think one of the best ways to deal with the emotions of trading is to read books by other successful traders." – Darrin Donnelly*

Eddie (Edward) Lampert was born on 19 July 1962, in New York, USA. He got inspiration to trade from his granny who was an avid investor. He used to sit with his granny while checking the performances of certain stocks.

When Eddie's dad died at a relatively young age, his mom, who used to be a full-time housewife, was forced to look for a job. He himself took up some odd jobs after school hours in order to ease the burden on his mom. Despite juggling school and odd jobs, he attained good grades. He was even able to participate in some extra-curricular activities and won an athlete award. With some effort on his part and financial assistance he received, he obtained a bachelor's degree in Economics with a first-class degree. That was in 1984.

In the same year, he began to work at Goldman Sachs and enjoyed a good career there. He later decided to start his own investment/trading business. One of his respected colleagues warned him against the possibility of failure in his business attempts.

He left that firm anyway; at the risk of failure. He was able to raise about $28 million and he was also introduced to new clients. He founded ESL Investments. He is also the chairman and CEO of Sears Holdings (SHLD). His firms have become a huge success, with Lampert himself making a personal income of $1.02 billion dollars in 2004. With a worth of $3.8 billion, he was the richest man in Connecticut. In 2006, he made an income of close to $1.5 billion.

He is married to Kinga Lampert and they are blessed with three children.

**Lessons**

These are the lessons that can be learned from Eddie's life and trading strategies:

1.  Some were inspired or encouraged to start trading by unusual persons. In Eddie's case, it was his granny that inspired him to start thinking about trading. Oddly enough, I was inspired by my maternal uncle who hadn't traded before, but who had seen successful traders. Some were inspired by their dads, friends, and so on. Who inspired/encouraged you to start trading?

2. Once again, your poor background or past shouldn't stop you from attaining financial freedom now or in future. Eddie's father was a lawyer, but his untimely death forced the family to start working hard to survive. Then, the future looked bleak. The fact that Eddie's dad wasn't around to pay for his education didn't stop him from earning a bachelor's degree at a prestigious school; neither did the fact stop him from becoming a multi-billionaire.

3. When Eddie Lampert wanted to leave the high-paying job he was doing at Goldman Sachs to found his own business, a colleague of his tried to discourage him. As you know, the majority of people think that it's better to do a job that guarantees a paycheck every week or month, than to rely on the uncertainties of the markets. Never be discouraged in trading. Although the profession is full of challenges, they can be overcome. Some traders have done this and they are living testimonies. Unusual people can also tell you to say 'bye-bye' to trading and go do something else. I was almost discouraged by someone whose opinions used to matter most to me in the past, but I'm thankful I didn't go back. It was a big surprise that a well-known founder of a very popular online trading education and information company announced some years ago that it was impossible to attain permanent success in Forex. Wasn't that very strange, a founder of a very popular Forex website telling people that they couldn't make it from Forex? The website is still very active. However, that statement shows that some of the so-called experts behind certain trading websites can't trade successfully on their own; yet they make the public believe that their websites can help people achieve their goals in the markets. Contrary to what "doubting Thomases" think, everlasting success is possible for traders.

4. Certain individuals have been denouncing Eddie as a bad CEO/investor. In spite of this, he is a victorious market player. When you become somebody, you will have many critics – some of whose criticism will be destructive rather than constructive. No matter what you do, some people will complain. Just let the complainers keep on doing their job while you continue doing your best and succeeding.

5. What about Eddie's investment strategies? He sells things at retail prices and buys them at wholesale prices. The cheaper the prices, the more bullish Eddie would be. He also doesn't hold too many positions at once: he only holds a few to several positions which have to do with the stocks he understands fully well. Rather than speculating on too many trading instruments that you don't fully understand, it's better for you to specialize on trading instruments that you understand very well, even if they are few. Over the time, you'll master them and make money with them.

6. Eddie believes that long-term performances are better than short-term results.

## Conclusion

Common sense is required in trading. This is one of the reasons why a robot cannot make consistent profits indefinitely. There are no perfect trading approaches, for wizards like Eddie lose sometimes. Orders ought to be placed logically, since no-one knows for sure what the market will do next. We all hate negativity, yet experienced traders know that it's an indispensable part of trading. We make gains in spite of negativity.

This chapter is concluded with a quote from Eddie Lampert:

*"You can't wait for an opportunity to become obvious… In investing, you constantly make decisions under conditions of uncertainty."*

# CHAPTER 11

# Maria Boyazny:
## An Influential Female Trader

*"You need to be comfortable with the level of risk you are taking when you trade." – Stuart McPhee*

Maria Boyazny is the Founder and Chief Executive Officer of MB Global Partners, which is based in New York. MB Global Partners is an asset management firm which focuses on the credit and special situations markets.

Maria earned a degree in Economics – with a concentration in Finance and minor in Mathematics (University of Pennsylvania). She later earned her MBA from Columbia University. She worked as a portfolio manager/managing director at Siguler Guff & Co. In addition, she has authored some books, spoken at conferences, and also been a guest speaker at Fox Business, CNN, Bloomberg TV, etc.

Maria has taken part in many prestigious professional career activities that distinguish her as a highly sought expert in the trading world. Her investment strategies are unique as well as effective. She makes consistent profits for her clients. Because of this, she has been recognized as one of the top five most influential women in hedge funds, among other accolades. Her firm's official website is: Mbglobalpartners.com.

**Lessons**

Here are some of the lessons you can learn from Maria Boyazny:

1.  The global markets are inefficient – in contrast to what some pundits believe. An individual trader/fund manager with decades of experience is a living testimony that the global capital markets are really inefficient.

2.  When you master the art of trading and the simple principles of everlasting success become your second nature, you'll find yourself trading effortlessly and making money. Maria trades without flinching and with the quiet confidence of somebody who knows what she is doing, what the markets are doing and how to take advantage of them. One person wrote that, for Maria, trading is as natural and effortless as breathing. She has reached a level at which she can no longer be swayed by market noises or fear of the future. Professional traders have reached that stage and you can reach it too.

3.  Managing over $4.5 billion for her clients, Maria's realized sizable returns for them, because she is able to do a simple thing: she makes consistent returns no matter what the markets are doing. The markets that slice the gamblers up are the markets that bring

great profits to the pros. It doesn't matter whether the markets go up or down; what matters is that you can harness gains from them no matter where they go. It's reported that many people lost their socks, shorts, shirts, sweats, homes, marriages and lives during the recent global financial crisis. However, astute traders like Maria identified this crisis early enough and make lots of money from it. You see, what brings loss for some is also what brings profit for others. For traders who know what they are doing, the trading business is really recession-proof.

4.  It's crucial to know how to pinpoint good trade setups and how to exit your orders properly. Please look for ways to know when to enter and when to exit.

## Conclusion

When we win, we may not learn any lessons. But when we lose, we learn valuable lessons that potentially make us better traders. You see, Smart Money has effective trading/investment rules that give them 'unfair' advantage over many other traders.

This chapter is ended with a quote from Maria Boyazny:

*"Many of the liquid credit assets such as high yield, might have a bit of room to run but overall are overpriced and investors need a gradual exit plan."*

# CHAPTER 12

# Tom Hougaard:
## A Superstar Trader/Investor

*"I have been taught the emotional pain of large losses when my ego wanted me to trade too big, and the pain of missing a huge move due to fear of entering a trade."*
*– Steve Burns*

Born in 1969, in Denmark, Tom Hougaard later moved to the United Kingdom in 1992, where he obtained a BA and MSc in Economics and Finance. He worked at Chase Manhattan Bank, but left the bank in 2000 to manage his personal portfolios. After that, he was employed by a brokerage company.

In 2002, he was chief market strategist at city index where he made copious market comments on popular media. He has also handled trading presentations and written many articles. In 2009, he started a website WhichWayToday.com where he posts premium articles, trading commentaries and runs a live trading room. The performances of the trading room have been very impressive.

Tom is a successful trader who's been showing others how to make money through his trading room services, articles and others. He owns a website named TraderTom.com. On that website, one can see some wonderful articles that reveal some of the greatest trading truths.

## Lessons

These are some of the lessons you can learn from Tom:

1.  One of the fastest ways to make money in the markets is to copy what successful traders are doing, either by social trading or trading rooms services or signals strategies services.

2.  There are money management, trade management, and risk management styles that are at variance with the mainstream ideas; yet they are successful in the markets.

3.  The extremely popular analytical tools like Fibonacci extension and retracement levels, Gann's line and grid, Elliot Waves, Andrew Pitchfork and some others are far from being the Holy Grail. In fact, many traders lose money with those popular tools in spite of them being venerated by the so-called gurus. The secrets to success don't lie in those analytical tools. Rather the secrets to success lie in what most traders can't do.

4.  Our mind is our enemy! This is true in most critical aspects of life as well as trading. We want good results and we're very enthusiastic about getting those results. Nevertheless, when it comes to facing the realities that have to do with the process of

getting those results, we compromise – we even give up. Those who want to start a strict program to lose weight aren't disciplined enough to deny themselves so that they can achieve their goals. Those who need to fast to achieve some spiritual and/or health goals quickly compromise when their body reacts violently to lack of food (we're addicted to food). Most of us can't stay away from foods and habits that are dangerous to our health. We want to go to the gym to stay fit, but we're reluctant to go when the time comes. We know it's bad to make/receive phone calls while driving, but we can't resist the temptation. We know what's good, but we find it more agreeable to do what's bad. The same is true of trading. We tend to do those things that aren't in our best interest as traders. We stay away from the markets or even quit trading altogether when we face challenges in the markets; whereas the way we deal with the challenges is what makes the difference between a successful trader and a failure who's no longer a trader. We hear sweet talks from those who motivate us to do exploits in life, including the markets, but we can't follow their recommendations. Tom says: "The chemical boost of imagining the outcome, to say the outcome out loud is essentially all the motivational speakers are facilitating to create success for themselves. Very few of them actually help people, not for the lack of trying, but because of who we human beings are. According to him, motivational talks are good enough to give us the feeling of achievement, but never take us to the full potential. One moment the mind is your friend, and the next moment it is the enemy, standing in the way of you achieving your goal. This is also true of trading.

5. When the trend changes, one needs to admit that and trade accordingly. It is not logical to think that the market will trend in a direction forever. We should be able to take advantage of the biases in the markets at any time. Great trading instruments must be cheap enough for buyers or expensive enough for sellers.

## Conclusion

Tom makes money in bear and bull markets, and you can do the same. It's worrisome that some traders still dread bear markets, while preferring only bull markets. Bear markets are also great for making money – you simply need to go short. A downtrend is usually accompanied by common dread and worry on the part of the speculator. This kind of reaction is not a surprise, for the average speculator doesn't think that the market may go bearish before it actually goes bearish. However, instead of staying out of a downtrend, one can employ trading approaches that work in bear markets.

This chapter concludes with a quote from Tom Hougaard:

*"However, the most important lesson I learned was why 99.9% of people fail at reaching their goals in life. We are addicted to pleasure and will avoid pain like the plague."*

# CHAPTER 13

# Michael Marcus:
## A Mentor to Trading Geniuses

*"You need to get comfortable with losing money, or you will never make money."*
*– Chris Tate*

Michael Marcus is a professional trader. He went to Johns Hopkins and studied Psychology at Clark University. He started speculating on the markets in 1972. His first trade was successful, though that might be out of pure luck. In 1973, his portfolio that was initially worth $24,000 was increased to $64,000. In fact, he is said to have turned his portfolio from $30,000 into $80 million.

Michael has worked for many trading firms in various capacities. His investment strategies are unique and the trading instruments he chooses are well-known and traded in well-planned ways. He is also a technical analyst. He is featured in a book called *The Predictors: How a Band of Maverick Physicists Used Chaos Theory to Trade Their Way to a Fortune on Wall Street*. He was reported to have been an ardent follower of the Maharishi Mahesh Yogi.

## Lessons

These are some of the lessons that can be learned from Michael:

1. Although Michael is today viewed as a legendary trader, he started as a noob who had initial challenges in the markets. You may be a noob today, but that shouldn't prevent you from becoming a legendary trader in future.

2. When Michael was having challenges, he was mentored by Ed Seykota (a market wizard). Ed's help and guidance made Michael a better trader. He was also taught money management. Do you find it difficult to be a successful trader? You might want to find a mentor who's a successful trader come talented coach. You might be surprised. Michael himself is now a mentor to professional traders.

3. There's life outside trading. Don't be a market addict – to the detriment of your spiritual, social, parental, connubial etc. health. That's what affected Jesse Livermore; the end of his life was worse. Michael was once making this kind of mistake. He was married to his screen and checked the market actions constantly, even at night. According to him, that was a factor that contributed to the collapse of his first marriage. He says: "If trading is your life, it is a torturous kind of excitement. But if you are keeping your life in balance, then it is fun. All the successful traders I've seen that lasted in the business sooner or later got to that point. They have a balanced life; they have fun outside of trading. You can't sustain it if you don't have some other focus.

Eventually, you wind up over trading or getting excessively disturbed about temporary failures." This is a great lesson.

4.  It's better to trades the markets that you understand very well and which you're comfortable with. Stay out of equilibrium markets, volatile markets, choppy and unpredictable markets. Trade only the markets that are easy to predict; the markets that you know very well. If you're only familiar with Forex markets, you'd have difficulty making money from trading futures. Stay out of irrational and insane markets and court sexy and trending markets. This is one way to increase the odds in your favour.

5.  Money management is very important. This is one of Michael's formulas for lasting survival in the markets. You can survive protracted losing streaks only when you risk a small amount per trade. When winning streaks come around, the losses are then recovered. By risking too much per trade, there's no way you can survive long in the markets; which means you won't be able to recover your losses and you'll stop trading. The best trading technique has losing streaks at times. With money management, you can avoid a margin call.

6.  We become better at trading only when we embrace losses and learn lessons from them. The lessons can change us for the better and revolutionize our trading approaches. Great traders don't think they will always win – that's impossible. We don't make progress when we blame the markets. We make progress when we learn from our mistakes.

7.  There are many ways to make money without being active on the markets. This may be through funds management accounts, social trading or signals strategy services. However, if you want to be a trader, you need to learn how to trade, including the trading approaches that fit your psychology. You need to discover the type of trader you are and what works for you.

## Conclusion

A good trader will eventually recover any recent losses she/he suffered. For examples, good funds managers have made gains that more than compensate for the negativity they experienced during the recent financial crises (some even made gains during the crises). It is also important to know which markets and currency trading instruments are favourable to your trading style. You need to begin to acquire the skills necessary to make you a victorious speculator. Should you fail to do this, you'd discover that you're still a novice in several years to come, just as you are now.

This chapter concludes with a quote from Michael:

*"Perhaps the most important rule is to hold on to your winners and cut your losers. Both are equally important. If you don't stay with your winners, you are not going to be able to pay for the losers."*

# CHAPTER 14

# Kenneth Griffin:
## Another Great Mr Trader

*"I've found that the more focused I am on trading and living a successful life, the fewer groups I actually fit into." – Louise Bedford*

Kenneth Griffin was born in 1968, Florida, USA. He is an American trader and funds manager. He attended Boca Raton Community High School, and then Harvard University. While at the University, he began to manage some portfolios (as well as focus on his education). His first portfolio was worth $265,000 (including contribution from his granny). He sold short and made gains from the markets in 1987.

As soon as he earned a degree in economics (1989), an investor named Frank C Meyer was impressed by his trading performance and he gave him $1 million to trade with. Kenneth was able to maintain his success with about 70% profit. Soon, people began to hear of his trading prowess and some were intrigued enough to start investing with him.

He founded his hedge fund firm, Citadel LLC, a Chicago-based investment firm, in 1990. The capital base was $4.2 million. The firm grew quickly. In fact, the business kept growing year after year and Kenneth grew richer and richer (year after year), until he eventually became a billionaire. He first appeared on Forbes 400 (2003), with a net worth of $650 million. His worth was eventually over $3 billion (some sources even say it has grown more than that). In 2011, he was ranked as the 512th richest person in the world.

In 2004, he earned an income of $240 million. He was paid $210 million in 2005, making him one of the 25 highest paid funds managers that year. His firm continued to perform strongly, and he was paid $1.7 billion in 2006, plus $2.6 billion in 2007. In 2011, he collected a salary of $700 million. No wonder he was able to buy the most expensive condo in Chicago for a mere $15 million, in 2012 (it was the most expensive there at the time). Very recently, he was paid close to $1 billion dollars.

At first he avoided the press and rarely gave interviews. But now, he is more open and has taken a glare of publicity. He now talks about his purchases, contributions and political views.

He makes large donations to various individuals and programs: including education, medicine, research and politics. For example, in February 2014, he gave $150 million to Harvard University, so that some students could receive financial assistance in their studies. That was the biggest single donation in Harvard's history, to date. The financial assistance is based on the needs of students, and helps some students who have difficulties in paying for their education.

Kenneth is happily married with two children.

**Lessons**

These are some of the lessons that can be learned from Kenneth Griffin:

1. Kenneth is a great trader, but without doubt, he has his own weaknesses. All traders have their strengths and weaknesses. The logic is to capitalize on your strengths and minimize/control your weakness. Doing so will push you ahead of the crowd who tend to be undisciplined in most cases.

2. The highest paid footballer in the world, Cristiano Ronaldo, is far poorer than the tenth highest paid funds manager in the world. In other words, the highest paid funds manager (David Tepper; Kenneth is number 5 on the 2014 list) is paid 35 times more than Cristiano Ronaldo. A footballer may be more popular because of hundreds of millions of fans and viewers worldwide; yet a funds manager, who trades on his computers in his office, may be far more strikingly rich. Kenneth was not born a billionaire, but he becomes one. His wealth is self-made. You may have been born in a financially humble family, but that shouldn't preclude you from reaching financial freedom.

3. I beg you profoundly; try to be the best trader you can be. Trading is full of challenges that can be overcome. Kenneth faced the challenges before him and he overcame them. You too can overcome. When you become a successful trader, you can manage others' money and you'll be paid handsomely when you make money for others. Your track record will speak for you.

The effort to reach consistency in trading may be daunting, but the eventual rewards are huge.

4.  Note that it took Kenneth many years to become what he is today; neither does he double his gains overnight. Please map out a long-term plan to make realistic and consistent gains each year. A trading career is a journey of a lifetime.

5.  Yes, Kenneth's beginning was humble. He started Citadel with a few million dollars and the firm grew up to become one of the world's largest hedge funds. The growth was gradual, but it was sure. Don't despise your small beginnings. They may be small but they can lead to great things.

6.  Leverage has advantages and disadvantages. It gives you some power while you're also exposed to more risk. The trick is to make use of the leverage you're given in a rational way so that you benefit from it and at the same time, limit the adverse effect it may bring.

## Conclusion

Please don't forget that our orders in the markets are expected to bring us some profits in the long run. So there is no need for us to stay glued to our computer; we'd do well to leave our orders to pan out without being micromanaged. As soon as we control our negativity, there will be recovery, and eventual going ahead.

This chapter concludes with a quote from Kenneth:

*"Capital markets reward you for what you learn that other people have yet to ascertain."*

# CHAPTER 15

# Israel Englander:
## Attaining Permanent
## Success in the Markets

*"When you are trading, trade the truth. Truth is the only safe ground to stand on." – Old Trader*

Israel Englander (sometimes called Izzy) is a hedge fund guru. He was born in 1948, in New York City, USA and was raised in a Jewish family – his parents were Poles who immigrated to the States after they left a Soviet labour camp. Israel became fascinated with the markets when he was in high school. He earned a BS (finance) from New York University in 1970. Later he applied for an MBA program at the same University and he was accepted, but he didn't finish his studies.

Before he enrolled for the MBA program, Israel worked at Kaufmann, Alsberg & Co, a Wall Street Firm. In 1985, he and his partner John Mulheren Jr founded an investment firm, Jamie Securities Co. The Belzberg family of Canada was a major investor in the firm, having contributed about $75 million. Mulheren was convicted of facilitating unlawful trading practices for Ivan Boesky (who was also a professional trader). Israel was never implicated with Mulheren's wrongdoings, but the lawsuit caused a very bad reputation that damaged Jamie Securities. The firm was shut down.

Israel and Ronald Shear founded Millennium Partners in 1989, with seed money of about $35 million. The beginning was very rough for the firm and as a result of this, Ronald Shear left the business. From that time on, Israel has made the firm a success, growing it into a very big hedge fund that is worth billions of dollars. Rather than charging a fixed management fee per annum, Israel shares trading expenses with his investors.

Now Millennium Management LLC, the firm uses several unique strategies to achieve its goals. It has about 900 employees and 12 offices and is one of the most successful hedge funds in the world. The firm trades with over $21 billion. In March 2014, Israel was worth $3.3 billion dollars. He has been very generous to Jewish schools and organizations. He is married to Caryl Englander and they have three children.

## Lessons

Here are some of the lessons you can learn from Israel Englander:

1.  Never give up when you face challenges in your career. When Israel and Ronald Shear founded Millennium Partners in 1989,

things were not encouraging then. Ronald even left him. Before all this, the Jamie Securities company he co-founded was dissolved. These things were enough for chickens who'd rather go back into their comfort zone. Nevertheless, Israel kept on rather than giving up and he ended up being the boss of one of the biggest and most successful hedge funds around.

2.  Israel is a good stock picker. He likes to pick promising stocks. It's what you pick that will bring gains for you. How can you find stocks and trading instruments that are really promising? You need to develop strategies that help you do this?

3.  Israel is secretive – even in the world of hedge funds. He doesn't appear in public, talk to the press, grant interviews or broadcast his photos. Yet, he has made billions of dollars from the markets. Really, those things aren't what will make you a successful trader. In fact, talking publicly about your open trades would have an adverse effect on your psychology because it would put your ego on the line. You don't have to be the most handsome, the biggest mouth, the greatest orator and the most hyped socialite before you can become a successful trader.

4.  Israel wasn't born rich, but he made fabulous money. His riches are self-made. No matter your background and economic class, you can end up making it in life.

5.  Are you often disturbed by your critics? Are your actions decided by what people say about you? It's a mistake to think you can always answer your critics, and in addition one of the best ways to fail is to try to please everybody. As a trader, just continue to put out your trading best and let others continue to make the noise. Despite a possibility of a hedge fund scandal and allegations of fraud affecting one of the traders at Millennium, Israel told his top employees that they shouldn't pay attention to

what they saw in the press, but they should focus on making profits so that they could keep their jobs.

6.  Israel's Millennium has been consistently successful. It makes an average of 17% returns per year: that certainly beats the bank. Good results were achieved when the markets were seriously unfavourable to the bulls and when the markets were seriously favourable to the bulls. With only a profit of one per cent per month, you can become rich in the long run – not only when you make 50% (that's a recipe for financial disaster). You can also make money in bull and bear markets.

7.  Like Israel, it's possible to attain permanent success in the market if you have strict risk management and realistic goals. At Millennium, trading is treated as serious business and no nonsense is allowed. There are many traders working for the firm and they must make money in order to retain their jobs. Each trader must also not experience drawdowns that go below the predetermined level, otherwise she/he is dismissed. On the other hand, traders who perform well at the firm is given more money to trade with. Prudent trading firms also employ effective risk control principles so as to ensure that they continue to enjoy everlasting triumph. By defining your maximum risk per trade, maximum roll-down per week or month (after which you temporarily stop trading for a while) and other risk control techniques like trailing stops, you survive the vagary of the markets.

## Conclusion

Formal education can't help protect our accounts as risk control principles can. Our discipline and sense of responsibility help us avoid approaches that can endanger our portfolios. When we started trading, we faced some recalcitrant challenges. If we'd done the right things from the beginning, the results could have been different. In order to move forward as traders, we try to focus on what we still have rather than what we have lost.

The quote below, which ends this chapter, is attributed to Israel:

*"Here's a chair and computer – go trade."*

# CHAPTER 16

# James Chanos:
## A Short Seller with Record Success

*"The most important function that fundamental short sellers bring to the market is that they are real time financial detectives." – James Chanos*

Born in 1975, James Chanos is an American professional speculator and funds manager who is a great bear in the market. He was born to a Greek family and he attended Yale. He worked as an analyst at Blyth Eastman Webber, Gilford Securities, and later, Deutsche Bank Capital Corp (where he was also vice president).

In 1985, James founded Kynikos Associates (registered in New York), which focuses on short selling. Since then he has amassed great wealth by making popular short trades. This is the mirror of what the Oracle/Sage/Wizard of Omaha, Warren Buffett, does, which is based on fundamentals and long-term bullish outlook. James Chanos uses fundamentals and long-term bearish outlook. He has successfully shorted some popular stocks like Baldwin-United and Enron Corporation, which have made him famous. He doesn't just sell short, he sometimes blows the whistle on some companies whose stocks, based on his analyses, would soon assume long-term southward journeys. He blew another whistle on China in 2010, that the country should be shorted. He had plausible reasons for saying this, but time will tell how true the forecast is.

How rich is James? A recent report reveals that he is worth about $1.5 billion. His net worth testifies to the validity of his forecasts and trading strategies.

**Lessons:**

These are some of the things that can be learned from James:

1. There are many profitable short sellers like James Chanos and Tim Knight. These are astute speculators who take advantage of bear markets while some buy-and-hold investors suffer. When a trading instrument moves south, that signifies that the bears are still willing to continue selling the seemingly undervalued market. Some of the profitable sell trades are also taken from bear markets that are already established; from the markets some people think are too cheap. Permabulls invariably suffer in weak markets – a stupid experience in such markets. In these weak markets, the permabulls pay dearly for prices that drop like stones. Why must you suffer in a bear market? You mustn't suffer at all when you have strategies that work in bull and bear markets. Of course, James also buys some stocks. He is sometimes bullish on stocks, with commendable success.

2.  Like James, you will do yourself a favour by undertaking intensive research into stocks you are interested in. By doing this, you'll get an insight into the probable reality that may affect your predetermined direction. Once your positions are open, you may want to hold them for as long as the markets are in your favour, like James who holds his positions for the long term. The big profits are to be made in the long-term.

3.  Sometimes, you may be correct in the long-term, but incorrect in the short-term. As a position trader or an investor, there are trade management techniques that can save you from being stopped out abruptly.

4.  According to James, you need to be able to weather being told you're wrong all the time. Critics may be jeering at you when your forecasts go wrong, but never mind. As long as your method has positive expectancy and you make more gains than you lose, you'll be fine.

5.  Don't be carried away by the noise the media make. When I was still a rookie, I checked several websites for technical and fundamental analyses on the instrument I wanted to trade. In most cases, I got lost among conflicting opinions. Even when I seemed to conclude that most analysts were saying the same thing, I still lost on the trade I made based on it. Don't worry about the noise in the market, even if you listen to it.

6.  It's better to start trading when one is a young man or woman. It was a regret that I started trading in my early 30s, not in my early or late 20s. In my article titled *Teach Your Teens the Art of Trading*, I mentioned some of the benefits of learning trading early in life. This is why some traders like Joe Ross, Anton Kreil, Peter Soodt, Kenneth Fisher, etc became financially free early. Elderly people can also learn trading and attain success in the market, but it's far better to do so when one is still young. This is what James says

further concerning this fact: "Life intrudes – as when you get older you end up with more responsibilities and your ability to take risk diminishes. If you are 25 and have a great idea and you fail, no one is going to hold it against you, and future employers and investors might actually look favourably upon it. So if you really want to pursue something, do it while you're young – you'll have more energy and you'll be able to take more financial and career risk. If it doesn't work, you still have your whole life ahead of you." Chanos thinks that if you have to take risk, take it early in life. Nevertheless, it's never too late for me; it's never too late for you.

## Conclusion

The bulls and the bears make the market what it is. Hence, the bulls and the bears are watching one another with suspicion and each group is ready to take advantage of the other group's stupidity. When the market experiences a roll-down, its existence may be transient, but the intensity may be great enough to make the bears wealthy.

This chapter is concluded by a quote from James.

*"There's a big difference between a long-focused value investor and a good short-seller."*

# CHAPTER 17

# Leon Cooperman:
## A Distinguished Trading Veteran

*"You have to respect the stock market. If you don't, you're going to get wiped out." – Leon Cooperman*

Leon G Cooperman was born on 25 April 1943, in New York, USA. He was born to Jewish parents who immigrated to the US. He is an astute American trader and philanthropist. He attended Hunter College and after graduation, he worked as a quality control engineer at Xerox. Later, he earned his MBA from Columbia Business School. That was 1967.

Immediately after leaving Columbia Business School, he started working at Goldman Sachs, serving that company in various capacities for the next 25 years. He then started a private firm called Omega Advisors, Inc, based in New York and managing about $6 billion.

In March 2013, Leon was worth $2.5 billion. Forbes has constantly ranked him among the most influential persons, the richest persons and the highest-earning funds managers. The Institutional Investor All-America Research Team survey voted him the best portfolio strategist for nine years. He belongs to various societies and foundations. As a philanthropist, he has made large donations towards many educational and cultural causes.

Leon's is married to a wonderful woman named Toby and they are blessed with children and grandchildren.

**Lessons**

Here are the lessons that can be learned from Leon Cooperman:

1. Leon's managed funds have been outperforming the markets for over 22 years. He makes average returns of at least 14.6% each year. This shows that when you have good strategies that can enable you to survive all market conditions, it is possible to make profits almost on an annual basis for the rest of your trading career, though some years can be better than others.

2. One secret of successful traders (including other professionals) is to employ the services of those who are more knowledgeable and more competent than they are. Leon is aware of this secret and makes use of it. In fact he likes to use this quote from Andrew Carnegie: "Here lies a man who was wise enough to bring into his service men who knew more than he." Hedge funds big boys and great financial institutions have pros who are working for them and thus contributing to their overall success.

3.  Leon uses fundamental analysis in his trading approaches and you can take note of this. Besides, you need to love trading and work hard at it. Discipline is also a must for traders who wish to attain success.

4.  There are always trading opportunities in the markets. Once the opportunities have been sighted, you can open your positions at the predetermined time. As an active trader, you need to monitor your trades and manage them properly.

5.  Leon likes to buy cheap markets and sell expensive markets. Some may call it contrarian trading – which works for those who are good at it. Profitable speculation also has to do with entering the markets when the prices are right for your positions.

6.  Large pullbacks (called crashes) are a normal thing in bull markets, and good speculators make money from them.

7.  Some of the stocks traded by Leon are winners and some of his stocks are losers, but he knows how to recover quickly and move ahead. This fact reflects in his account history. You can't be right all the time, but with good trading management principles, you can always recover at last and move ahead.

8.  There are chart patterns, market cycles and repetitive trends in the markets, which have very high winning probabilities. This is one of the secrets behind Leon's success. You need to identify cycles and repetitive chart patterns that work for the financial instruments you trade.

9.  Courage is important for traders. You need to believe in your trading approach, especially if they worked for you in the past. Sometimes, things may not go as expected, but with persistence, you will rebound. You don't need to abandon your proven system because of temporary losing streaks.

10. Trading is a university from which you can't graduate. You continue to learn new things that can improve your career more and more. Leon said: "One thing nice about the investment business is that, even though I'm 68, I continue to learn. You learn something every month and every quarter."

## Conclusion

There isn't a trader without a scar; and the scar of every trader is the sacrifice being made now and then. Success comes at a cost. Your victory doesn't lie in *knowing* what it takes to become a profitable speculator; your victory lies in *doing* what it takes to become a profitable speculator.

This chapter is concluded by this quote:

*"I think all we've learned is what we already knew, is that stocks have become like commodities, regrettably, and they go up to a limit and they go down to a limit. And we've also known over the years that when they go down, they go down faster than they go up."*

# CHAPTER 18

# Victoria Grimsley:
## A World Trading Champion

*"The markets don't care about your background, your gender or your age. It's one of the only platforms in the world that offers you a limitless stage to refine your art."* – *Louise Bedford*

Victoria Grimsley is a dancer, singer and actress in Los Angeles, California, USA. She is also a successful trader who won the Robbins Trading World Cup Championships in 2013, which makes her a world trading champion. She won that contest by generating an annual return of 160% (net profits), thus receiving the trophy. Each year, contestants register with a minimum of $10,000 and trade it for one year. A man named Song Li (American-Chinese) came second with an annual return of 119%; while another man named Rene Wolfram (Germany) came third with an annual return of 53%.

Victoria is raising two young boys.

## Lessons

What can we learn from Victoria?

1.  Women should never underestimate your right to become a trader, including your limitless potential to become financially free. Victoria isn't the first woman to win the Robbins Trading World Cup Championships – she's the second; Michelle Williams was the first in 1997. Michelle is a daughter of Larry Williams (a super trader that will soon be featured in an article in this series). It's very sad that some people still underestimate women when it comes to online trading. It's unfair to underestimate women in the trading world because there's no level of achievement that can't be attained by them. In fact, women like Victoria Grimsley and other female traders have been a blessing to the trading world. In addition, they are a source of inspiration and encouragement to us.

2.  Based on the quote at the end of this chapter, it's clear that Victoria is very passionate about trading. Successful traders have highly developed skills, and a strong drive for mastery and discipline. Good trading approaches need to be followed religiously, without irrational discretion. You need to do this so as to be successful too.

3.  Contrary to what some critics say, technical indicators work in the markets. Although it doesn't work always, just like the strategies advocated by the critics. Victoria uses MAs, candlesticks, Parabolic SAR and other analytical tools, which she

decided to adopt after years of testing. These are the analytical tools that she used to win the contest – evidence that they work!

4.  Victoria is a trend follower. She looks for a dominant bias and follows it for as long as it's intact. You don't need to go against the dominant bias in an effort to prove that your strategy is correct. The markets don't have mercy on foolish traders.

5.  Being busy with other activities and professions shouldn't necessarily preclude you from trading. Victoria is an active dancer, actress, singer, mother, etc., but she is still able to trade successfully, balancing everything. Indeed, what you're currently doing shouldn't preclude you from accessing the riches the markets proffer. You can combine trading with other activities and still live a balanced life.

6.  Contrary to what the public believes, successful trading isn't fictitious: it's real. It is real people that open real trades in the markets and they make real profits.

7.  In trading championships as well as individual trading, high risk isn't advisable. In trading contests like Robbins Trading World Cup Championships, a typical participant may make 500% returns over a short period of time, only to drop far behind, or even receive a margin call. Those who target several hundreds of percentage returns very fast won't definitely last long in the markets.

## Conclusion

We believe it's possible to make profits in the markets, and that can be done consistently on an annual basis. What you don't believe, you don't get empowered to become. We don't care what causes the beginning of a long-term bias in a market. What matters is that we profit from the bias, without knowing why the bull and the bear take their positions. Many people make money from long-term biases, and certain people lose; but a determined trader will not quit. If a horse throws off a determined rider, she or he will mount it again.

This chapter ends with a quote from Victoria:

*"I love to do things that keep my creative juices flowing, and I believe trading has a lot of creativity in it. I am 100% devoted to trading."*

# CHAPTER 19

# Dan Loeb:
## The Kanye West of Wall Street

*"To me, the freedom to be able to work when and where I want to is even more important than the money. This freedom is, of course, easy to attain by working as a trader." – Ruediger Born*

Daniel S Loeb was born on 18 December 1961, in Santa Monica, California, USA. He was born to Jewish parents. His father was a partner at a law firm, while his mother was a historian. He went to the University of California, but graduated from Columbia University, earning a degree in economics. He became fascinated by the market at a very young age, and made a profit of $120,000 from his stock market investment while still at the University. However, the profit was forfeited in another venture, which, needless to say, taught him a special lesson.

From 1984 to 1987 he worked at Warburg Pincus. He worked as a director at a record label, after which he worked as a risk arbitrage analyst at Lafer Equity Investors. He worked at Jefferies LLC from 1991 to 1994. He then worked as a specialist at Citigroup.

In 1995, he founded Third Point Partners LLC with just $3.3 million. He reveals his feelings when starting at that time, and I quote him: "I almost got stage fright the day before I started the fund. I had five or six family members and a few friends and $340,000 of my own money, which was my life savings from ten years working on Wall Street."

Many years later, in 2013, he is featured among the 40 wealthiest funds managers. This shows that his investment strategies have been working for him. The portfolio that is being managed by his New York-based company is now worth $14 billion.

Dan has been famous for his letters, which he writes to company executives, criticizing them for poor management decisions which are against the interests of shareholders. Some of the letters have been effective enough to cause changes in the companies' executives. His tactic is to invest in a company, increasing his stake considerably so that he can have his say in the company. For example, he initiated an effective attempt to remove Scott Thompson as chief executive officer at Yahoo!, replacing him with Marissa Mayer.

As of April 2014, Dan Loeb himself is worth $2.2 billion. He is married to Margaret Davidson Munzer. He likes to surf in the Caribbean and Indonesia.

He is involved in many programs that have to do with philanthropy, education, human rights, politics, military, medical research, industry and the arts; either participating or donating generously. In return, he has been honoured with awards.

**Lessons:**

These are some of the lessons you can learn from Dan:

1. The markets are a level playing field. They don't respect your place in society. Yes, as Dan puts it: "'One's place in society' does not matter at all. We are a bunch of scrappy guys from diverse backgrounds (Jewish, Muslim, Hindu etc.) who enjoy outwitting pompous asses like yourself in financial markets globally." Our ethnic or religious background doesn't matter. What matters is that we want to be successful market speculators that are smarter than most others.

2. Dan loves to bet on the markets that most others are afraid to invest in. He purchases stocks at companies that look hopeless, and then effects radical changes in the management of the companies and helps them become profitable again. Dan cares about making money for his investors, and he does everything possible to realize the goals. Our stakeholders and investors' interests should have preponderance over our personal interests and motives.

3. You need to adopt trading principles that work – even becoming philosophical about them. You need to know that opportunities to make money arise from chaos and imbalance in the markets. How do you then make money from that? Look for a good strategy that has high probability setups.

4. Good trading principles are also helpful in normal life. Traders think and act like traders. For example, a good trader may translate the discipline and emotional control she/he accomplishes in trading to life outside trading as well. Traders

ought to be diligent and hardworking, having the tenacity and grit, enjoying what they do with great passion.

5. When we follow our time-tested rules and lose, it is better than when we violate our time-tested rules and win. We don't make mistakes when we follow our rules (even if we lose with them), we make mistakes only when we violate our rules. About this Dan says that he wants people with good processes and good outcomes, but he would rather have somebody working for him who had a good process and a bad outcome in a given year than somebody with a bad process and a good outcome.

6. Timing is everything in the markets. How often have you opened orders, only to see that the market moves in your favour after you've been stopped out? Look for ways to improve your timing. One method is to join an uptrend during a pullback; and vice versa for a downtrend.

7. When you become really good at trading, you will become good at pattern recognition and identification of historical trends/cycles. The ability to do this comes from experience you gain from looking at charts. Some wrongly call this "instinct."

8. Super trades aren't infallible. We can be sure that we'll make mistakes, since we don't have answers to everything, nor are we perfect. We should bear this in mind when we make losing trades. But this shouldn't deter us from being profitable.

9. Leverage is good when used judiciously, but very dangerous when used illogically. When you make a profit of 20% per annum as a result of risking 0.5% of your account per trade, and another person generates a profit of 40% or 60% per annum out of risking 1% or 1.5% per trade, do you think the other person is a smarter trader? The answer is NO! It's just that the other person has achieved higher returns by betting bigger per trade,

thus increasing her/his risk of higher drawdowns. With that, the person can also suffer about 50% or 70% drawdowns. Therefore the best trading method is to look for ways to optimize profits with as few drawdowns as possible. Dan has made big improvements in this area since 2008.

10. Traders and investors should look for opportunities the world over. The American markets are still the biggest, most important, and most profitable (with arguably the best companies and capital markets), but there are increasing opportunities in other countries like India, China, Brazil, etc. You miss wonderful opportunities to make profits if you ignore these countries.

11. For you to make money, you must be willing to take risks. There is no way to tap the riches in the markets unless you become a trader or investor. People go into trading because they think they can become rich quickly, but it's better to be realistic than idealistic. A healthy appetite for risk involves effective risk management.

## Conclusion

We may not fully understand all the forces behind market actions. For example, pullbacks in weak markets may be stronger than pullbacks in strong markets, but we can make money in these kinds of price actions. When gaining more and more experience as speculators, we become more effective at controlling risk – and our rewards also increase accordingly. Please see the quote below. Super traders aren't infallible gods that predict the markets accurately. Rather, they are experts who are good at taking opportunities. Trading principles that work are timeless and they don't change with changing market conditions and the time.

This chapter is ended by a quote from Dan:

*"I have never professed to have a crystal ball that forecasts market direction...*
*The secret to our success is congruence between our investment style and my*
*personal investment style and philosophy, the fundamental elements of which have*
*remained constant over almost 18 years."*

# CHAPTER 20

# Barry Rosenstein:
## Why He Spends Money As He Likes

*"By now, most private investors know that there are some grandmasters in the world of finance. It would be considered poor form not to emulate these... industry superstars." – Jens Rabe*

We want to take a closer look at a hedge fund titan – Barry Rosenstein. He is the man who owns a record $147 million mansion. He is a self-made billionaire who made his fortune from the markets. He obtained Bachelor of Arts/Science degree at Lehigh University in 1981 and got his MBA at University of Pennsylvania Wharton School in 1984.

He worked as an investment banker at Merrill Lynch and was then hired by Asher Edelman. He has been investing huge amounts of money for decades. Before he founded Jana Partners hedge fund in 2001, he worked at several other firms. Since he founded Jana Partners, he has been making around 23% profits per annum. Jana Partners now manages $7.5 billion dollars. He's become highly paid; for instance, he was recently paid $250 million in one year, and he is now worth at least $1.3 billion.

A lover of yoga, Barry lives in New York, USA. His wife is Lizanne Rosenstein and he has children.

## Lessons

These are some of the lessons that can be learned from Barry:

1.  Barry's beginnings were humble, but it didn't take him long to become very rich. He made his vast fortune from the markets. One thing is sure: you too can become very rich as a result of your activities in the markets.

2.  His vast fortune stemmed from making decent profits per annum, not from doubling his accounts now and then. For example, he made 16% on Jana portfolio in 2006, plus another 17% in the firm's small cap. He is considered a genius not because he makes hundreds of percentage per annum.

3.  Barry is one of the richest men in America and has made professional and personal purchases, some of which have made him unpopular. He once bought a duplex apartment at 15 Central Park West at $29 million and spent another million to refurbish it according to his standards. He made another purchase as one source puts it, and I quote, "Money can buy you more than just stuff: It all took only eight months to complete. All this pales, of course, next to Rosenstein's purchase early this

month of a Hamptons home for $147 million – the most ever paid for a private residence in the United States. The 18-acre beachfront property has an elaborate garden that was the dream of its former owner, the late Christopher H Browne, complete with foot paths and bridges over a pond." Since he doesn't like the spotlight he gets for his extravagant spending, he plans to spend a further $60 million on another apartment in Manhattan. Several years ago, one billionaire gave cash gifts totalling $3 million to his ten favourite actresses and actors. That means each actress/actor got a cash gift of $300,000. The billionaire was criticized by the public for wasting money on a very small minority, while there were many causes and people that needed financial assistance. The fact is that everyone is free to spend their money as they like. The money belongs to him and he chooses how to spend it; just as you have the right to spend your money as you like. Many people want to be financially free but they can't do what it takes to attain financial freedom. They want to prosper, but they don't have the patience, perseverance and tenacity that can help them achieve their goals. Are these not the people that give online trading a bad image? Now, someone refused to be discouraged, working his way to financial freedom in spite of the challenges that people want to avoid, and they are now telling him how to spend his money. Whether or not you spend your money as people want, you can't take your riches to the grave. Let Barry continue to enjoy his money while those who criticize him ponder how to start their own journey towards financial freedom. At least, it doesn't pay to keep your fingers crossed while criticizing successful people. That can't put food on your table. One of the ways to financial freedom is online trading. Please start your own journey and when you become very rich, you can spend your money as you like.

4.  One of Barry's areas of interests is called shareholder activism, which has now become very well known. This is a system in

which wealthy funds managers demand radical rehabilitation in the companies they are interested in; they will invest heavily in a publicly-traded company and then demand financial and managerial changes.

## Conclusion

The markets offer riches that can't be accessed unless you become a trader or an investor. Despite your trading experience, you must stand your ground in determination, no matter the challenges and uncertainty in the markets. Refuse to give up or give in to the pressure to quit. Imagine if setting a goal for yourself, you plan to make a certain percentage within a month or a quarter, but you ended up reaching that goal only after six months or one year; don't feel bad. Instead, say, "I'll meet the goal sooner next time." You don't need to be discouraged simply because you fail to meet a goal for a period of the time.

This chapter ends with by a quote from Barry:

*"I prefer to work behind the scenes and not have a public battle."*

# CHAPTER 21

# Larry Williams:
## From $0.01 Million to Over $1.1 Million

*"According to a popular drink advert in the UK, good things come to those who wait. Trading is no different. It takes time and practice to become a consistently profitable trader. But when you do get there, everything will become very easy." –*
*Max Munroe*

Larry Williams is a very brilliant American trader, author and researcher. He was born on 6 October 1942, in Miles City, Montana, USA. He graduated from Billings Sr High, in Billings, Montana, in 1960. He also graduated from the University of Oregon, Eugene; being a student of journalism. While at school he was very active in sports. He also belonged to Honorary Professional Fraternity (Alpha Delta Sigma), in which he was a notable member.

He has written at least 11 popular books on trading and other important topics. He created many popular indicators like Williams Percentage Range, COT indices, cycle forecasts and others. With his loyal friend Louis Mendelsohn, who is also a trader and software developer, he has created new cutting-edge analytical tools.

In 1987, Larry Williams was the winner of World Cup Championship of Futures Trading from the Robbins Trading Company. He turned $10,000 million to over $1.1 million in twelve months. That reflected over ten thousand and nine hundred percent returns. He was given an award by the MTA (the Market Technicians Association) in 2014. He also funds a scholarship that is available to the University of Oregon students of journalism and communication who are creative, but may not have a high GPA.

Larry has been involved in various forms of activities, including politics, charities, researches, trading seminars around the globe and so on and so forth. His website is Ireallytrade.com.

**Lessons:**

Here are some of the lessons that can be learned from Larry.

1.  You're already a trader, according to Larry. How true is this statement! You buy or sell wheat. You travel and exchange currencies. You buy and sell houses. You offer goods for sale, or you buy goods. The list can go on endlessly. You're already a trader; though in a different sense. Why can't you then go professional and tap the riches the markets offer you? Larry lives the life many people can only dream of. He lives in the US Virgin Islands, writes, does research and enjoys trading.

2.  Let's look at the quote at the beginning of this chapter. It is from Max Munroe, and it says that when one masters the market, one will discover that trading is easier than is thought. This

profession has a bad public image because people think it's extremely difficult to make consistent profits in the market. It is true that this is difficult for those who don't know what they are doing. The solution to the problem in the art of trading is simple indeed.

3.   Larry has been trading for more than 50 years. His lasting career means that it is possible to attain a lasting success in your career as a trader.

4.   As far as Larry is concerned, trading excellence runs in his family. Ten years after he won Robbins Trading World Cup Championship, his daughter Michelle (Academy Award Nominee) won the same championship. That was 1997. His son Dr Jason Williams, who is a psychiatrist at Johns Hopkins, wrote a book called *The Mental Edge in Trading*, which documents the personality of successful market speculators. Do you want trading excellence to run in your family? Do you want your spouse, your children and so on to become successful in the markets? Do you want your children to be richer than you?

5.   Part of his secret is seasonal patterns and market cycles. These things work for traders who know how to take advantage of them. Please go learn about them.

6.   Yes, people can learn to trade. Just like any other profession, trading is an art that can be taught. If you're interested, you may want to look for a great coach to show you the way. One thing that is special about Larry – unlike most other coaches – is that he doesn't just coach; he trades. Larry has been an educator for just as long as he has been a trader. There are many coaches out there who can't trade profitably over the long term, but there are coaches like Larry who can, and do, trade profitably. Larry himself said: "When I teach people how to day trade I put my own hard cash at risk, so you can really see how it works. I have

traded $1,000,000 in front of students and gave them back 20% of the profits." These are the people that are recommended for those who want to learn how to become wining market speculators.

7.  Price is king. It's the most important indicator and the final arbiter. The bulls and the bears may fight and disagree, but price is the one that will tell who's right or wrong.

## Conclusion

Top traders know they are victorious only because they accept their errors. That's why they are victorious. Accepting errors make them rich, since they also get battered by the uncertainties in the markets. They can be adversely affected by unforeseen crashes and rallies. They can lose money in foreign markets (or make money). Their timing may sometimes be wrong, and they may even invest in the wrong stocks. But instead of accepting defeat, they mentally recovered. They aren't bothered with a positive or a negative trade. These great speculators are very good at accepting negative trades, making uncertainties their ally and facing negativity victoriously. That's why they are rich.

This chapter ends with a quote from Larry:

*"If you are not yet making money, what do you do? Go back to the basics! My bet is that you have not learned what moves markets . . ."*

## CHAPTER 22

# Toby Crabel:
## A Famous Contrarian Trader

*"When it comes to playing the markets. After all, it's all about making money, not about being right." – JC Parets*

Toby Crabel is an American trader who's made himself successful by his own efforts. He studied finance at the University of Central Florida. He got his feet wet in the markets while still a student. He was even a professional tennis players for a few years.

Toby has written many articles about short-term patterns in trading. In 1992 he worked as a trader for Victor Niederhoffer in New York. After leaving Niederhoffer he undertook a series of speculative activities. In 1998, he began to run his own funds from his residence, and he has been making decent profits since then. The Financial Times has referred to him as "the most well-known trader on the counter-trend side."

His firm, Crabel Capital Management, LLC, has been ranked among the big funds with nice profits. His website is Crabel.com. According to the website, Crabel Capital Management is a global alternative investment firm specializing in futures and foreign currency trading. Pioneers of short-term, systematic trading, the firm has evolved over the last two decades to offer broadly diversified, unique products that are valuable complements to sophisticated portfolio design. Crabel Capital Management has delivered over 20 years of uncorrelated returns to its worldwide customer-base. For example, the firm made a profit of 16.7% in 2005. The assets under management are about $3.2 billion, and there are many employees working at the firm.

In 1990 he wrote a helpful book called *Day Trading with Short-term Price Patterns*.

## Lessons

These are some of the lessons that can be learned from Toby Crabel:

1. Toby is referred to as a self-made millionaire, meaning that he didn't inherit millions, but he made millions for himself. In fact, he is a multi-millionaire. You can make yourself successful by your own efforts as a trader. You can work your own miracle of financial freedom, tapping from the riches the markets offer all of us.

2. He is a living testimony that it's possible to make consistent profits from the markets. For many years, he has made profits on annual basis. It's clearly possible to not have a red year as a trader, and therefore it's imperative that you find a way to achieve the goal of attaining green years successively. I admit that

some years will have more profits than others, like making 35% last year and only 11% this year, like making 5% last year and making 23% this year, but a red year can be avoided. If you haven't achieved this goal, then you've got a job to do. Toby Crabel is a human being like you.

3. Please see the quote at the end of this chapter. Risk is best controlled by taking a large number of small trades versus making a few large bets on a small number of trades."

4. Trend following works, and so do contrarian trading systems (especially the ones with good expectancy). There are no everlasting trends in the markets, which means there will always be turning points. These turning points tend to surprise many people while bringing satisfactory rewards to those who correctly anticipate the turning points and capitalize on them. Some turning points may be temporary pullbacks which would be strong while they last and some pullbacks may portend the beginning of new protracted biases. The best mix is to know when to follow the trend and when to go against it.

## Conclusion

It's very interesting when one knows how to trade deceptive price movement, since price sometimes moves very furiously against the majority and nets some contrarian traders huge gains. The reason for occasional contrarian moves is clear, for many who have gone long because of a transient rally have quickly smoothed their positions and then entered the market again as a result of a sharp dip in price. The recalcitrant bulls who stubbornly stick to their positions are either getting stopped out or are being forced to close their portfolios; otherwise they'd suffer more devastating damage. When a deceptive bullish movement becomes a snare to the unwary traders, the trader sells in a hurry and thus causes further dip in the market.

This chapter is concluded by a quote taken from Crabel website (Crabel.com):

*"Our core trading philosophy is that strategies should capture enduring and explainable market participant behaviour... We also think that risk is best controlled by taking a large number of small trades versus making a few large bets on a small number of trades."*

# CONCLUSION

"Twenty years from now you will be more disappointed by the things you didn't do than by the ones you did," said Mark Twain. Poverty has become widespread and it's bound to continue increasing globally. Think about your loved ones and your future. Think about your children and your financial security when you become old. Do you want your child to be richer than you? Please think about teaching your child the art of trading, for it doesn't hurt if she/he becomes the wealthiest person in your family.

Trading is one of the greatest jobs and one of the highest paying jobs in the world, but it's also one of the most challenging. When the challenges are overcome, honestly, things can become easier than thought. Our breakthrough begins in a new direction, for speculation is a fantastic lifestyle in which our brains help us make money and our self-control helps us remain permanently successful.

Those who keep on making an effort to reach profitability in the market will inevitably reach a stage when they start making money effortlessly and consistently. These are the people that the public call "market wizards," "super traders," "pros," "expert speculators," "gurus," "witches," "mad geniuses," etc. The public think something is special about them, but these people know that there's nothing special about them. They are consistently profitable because of their many years of experiences, plus their winning speculation principles have been practiced again and again until they become their second nature. You think they are smarter, more brilliant, more fortunate, more intelligent, and more innovative. Nevertheless, they don't think they are better than you. What makes the difference is that they decided to continue fighting for success at the stage that most others quit.

Thank you for reading this book. May you become a successful trader.

# ABOUT THE AUTHOR

Azeez Mustapha is a trading professional, funds manager, an InstaForex official analyst, a blogger at ADVFN.com, and a freelance author for trading magazines. He works as a trading signals provider at various websites and his numerous articles are posted on many websites such as www.ituglobalforex.blogspot.com.

Contact: azeez.mustapha@analytics.instaforex.com.

# ALSO BY AZEEZ MUSTAPHA

# LEARN FROM THE GENERALS OF THE MARKET

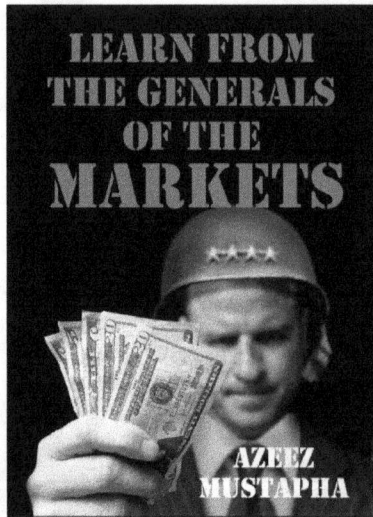

If you want to win on the trading battlefield, you need the right ammunition.

Trading is like any other profession: to succeed, you need to arm yourself with the necessary skills. Enter the arena without knowing what you are doing, and you are sure to lose your money.

You need help from the experts.

*Learn From the Generals of the Markets* profiles twenty renowned super traders from around the world, great traders who know what it takes to be successful in the markets. The book gives an overview of their careers and explains what lessons can be drawn from their success, so you can apply their methods and techniques to your own trading. It will help you gain the expertise you need to improve your prospects.

This essential guide should be part of every trader's armament.

Available in paperback and for the Kindle.

## MORE BOOKS FROM ADVFN

# HOW TO MAKE BIG MONEY TRADING IN ALL FINANCIAL CONDITIONS

### by Simon Watkins

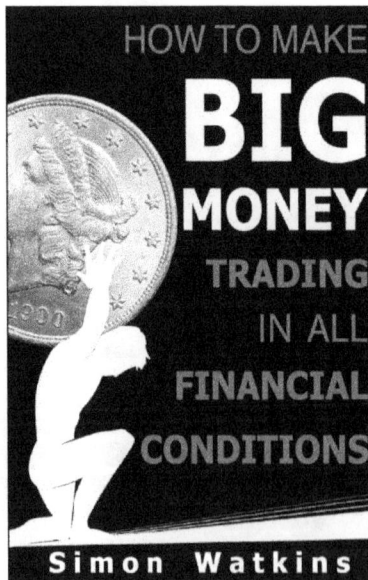

The markets are going through a period of turbulence right now, but even in periods of low market volatility there's always some asset, somewhere in the world, that oscillates in price sufficiently to offer traders opportunities to make big money. The trick is to know what the asset is, to identify whether it's trading higher or lower than it should be, and to have the skill, speed of thought and tenacity to take advantage of it.

In the follow up to his book *Everything You Need To Know About Making Serious Money Trading The Financial Markets*, Simon Watkins covers changing volatility patterns, risk-on/risk-off trading, how to find value in emerging markets and long-term global economic cycles. He outlines more fundamental principles that should guide your trades and trading methodologies to help you succeed.

Fully illustrated with detailed charts, the book shows how you can use technical analysis to make your decisions, how to manage your risk and how to take out hedge positions to offset possible losses.

Available in paperback and for the Kindle.

# EVERYTHING YOU NEED TO KNOW ABOUT MAKING SERIOUS MONEY TRADING THE FINANCIAL MARKETS

### by Simon Watkins

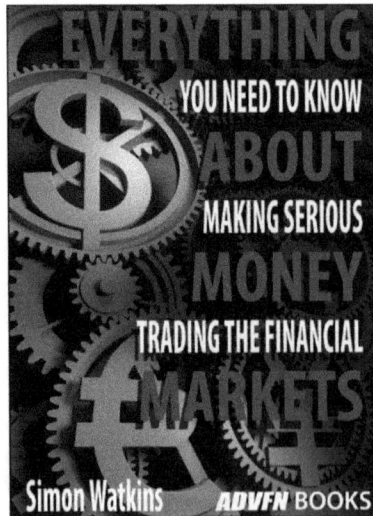

All over the world, people are trading on the financial markets. Some of them make a fortune – and many more lose their shirts. This book tells you how to be one of the winners.

It's a stark and sobering fact that around 90% of retail traders lose all of their trading money within about 90 days. That's because they have little grasp of the realities, technicalities, psychology and nature of the financial markets. In short, they don't know what they are doing.

*Everything You Need To Know About Making Serious Money Trading The Financial Markets* teaches you how to avoid being one of the 90%, and explains how to stack the odds firmly in your favour so you can become one of the 10% that make life-changing money trading. It's a trading bible that covers all aspects of the subject, from the psychology of trading and the mindset you need to succeed, through the fundamental principles that should guide your trades, to the trading methodologies that will help you succeed.

Fully illustrated with detailed charts, the book shows how you can use technical analysis to make your decisions, how to manage your risk and how to take out hedge positions to offset possible losses.

Available in paperback and for the Kindle.

# 101 CHARTS FOR
# TRADING SUCCESS

**by Zak Mir**

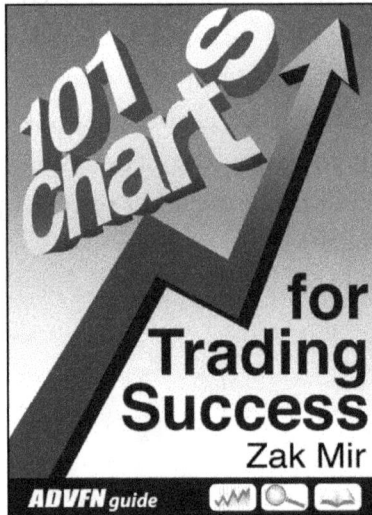

Using insider knowledge to reveal the tricks of the trade, Zak Mir's *101 Charts for Trading Success* explains the most complex set ups in the stock market.

Providing a clear way of predicting price action, charting is a way of making money by delivering high probability percentage trades, whilst removing the need to trawl through company accounts and financial ratios.

Illustrated with easy to understand charts this is the accessible, essential guide on how to read, understand and use charts, to buy and sell stocks. *101 Charts* is a must for all future investment millionaires.

Available in paperback and for the Kindle.

# THE GAME IN WALL STREET

**by Hoyle and Clem Chambers**

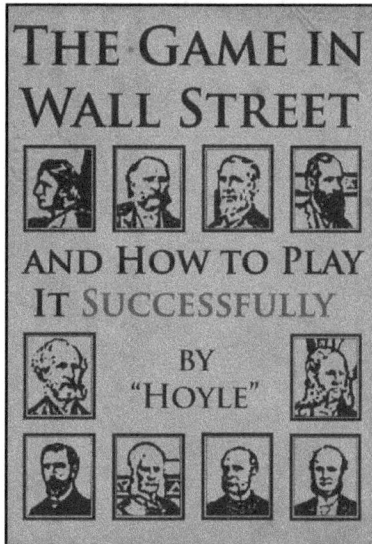

As the new century dawned, Wall Street was a game and the stock market was fixed. Ordinary investors were fleeced by big institutions that manipulated the markets to their own advantage and they had no comeback.

*The Game in Wall Street* shows the ways that the titans of rampant capitalism operated to make money from any source they could control. Their accumulated funds gave the titans enormous power over the market and allowed them to ensure they won the game.

Traders joining the game without knowing the rules are on a road to ruin. It's like gambling without knowing the rules and with no idea of the odds.

*The Game in Wall Street* sets out in detail exactly how this market manipulation works and shows how to ride the price movements and make a profit.

And guess what? The rules of the game haven't changed since the book was first published in 1898. You can apply the same strategies in your own investing and avoid losing your shirt by gambling against the professionals.

Illustrated with the very first stock charts ever published, the book contains a new preface and a conclusion by stock market guru Clem Chambers which put the text in the context of how Wall Street operates today.

Available in paperback and for the Kindle.

# THE DEATH OF WEALTH

**by Clem Chambers**

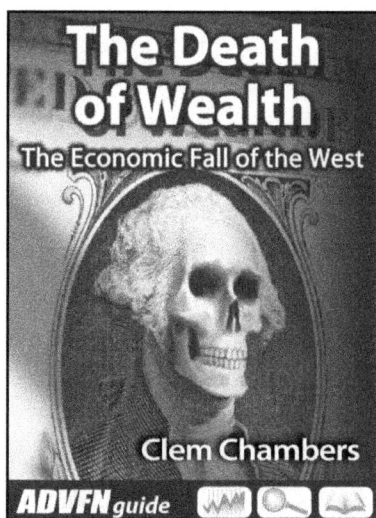

Question: what is the next economic game changer?
Answer: The Death of Wealth.

Market guru Clem Chambers dissects the global economy and the state of the financial markets and lays out the evidence for the death of wealth.

*The Death of Wealth* flags up the milestones on the route towards impending financial disaster. From the first tentative signs of recovery in the UK and US stock markets at the start of 2012, to the temporary drawing back from the edge of the Fiscal Cliff at the end, the book chronicles the trials and tribulations of the markets throughout.

Collecting together articles and essays throughout the last twelve months along with extensive new analysis for 2013, *The Death of*

*Wealth* allows us to look at these tumultuous events collectively and draw a strong conclusion about what the future holds.

2012 started with the US economy showing signs of recovery, and European financial markets recovering some of the ground lost during the euro crisis. It ended with Obama's re-election and the deal that delayed the plunge off the fiscal cliff by a few months.

In between, the eurozone crisis continued, but none of the affected countries actually left the eurozone; quantitative easing tried to turn things around with the consequences of these 'unorthodox' actions yet unknown; and the equity markets after the mid-year correction became strongly bullish.

*The Death of Wealth* takes you through the events of 2012 month by month, with charts showing the movements of the FTSE 100, the NASDAQ COMPX and the SSE COMPX throughout the year.

With an introduction by renowned market commentator and stock tipster Tom Winnifrith and a summary by trading technical analyst Zak Mir, this collection chronicles the rocky road trip the financial systems of the world have been on and predicts the ultimate destination: the death of wealth as we know it.

Available in paperback and for the Kindle.

For more information, go to the ADVFN Books website at www.advfnbooks.com.

**ADVFN BOOKS**